Shut up and Listen

Jennifer L. Risley

INKS & BINDINGS

Inks and Bindings
888-290-5218
www.inksandbindings.com
orders@inksandbindings.com

Contents

Introduction:

Life

Life is a funny word

In a way it tells you the basics of how to live

Look at the letters in the word "Life"

Notice the arrangements of the letters

In the middle of the word "Life" there is the word "if"

How many people have asked themselves, "What

if" I had waited five more minutes?"

Or, "What if I didn't go to the movies that night?"

If you take our the letter 'F' in the word

"Life" you'd have the word "Lie"

If we question our lives and made our decisions

all over again already knowing the outcome of

those choices, our lives would be a "lie"

Life is a series of choices, decisions, and events that

help to define who we are as individuals

If we were to change that, we would change who we are

Our lives would be a lie we'd no longer be what we thought

we were or be the same person that people think we are

Chapter One:
Families

It all starts with that. Without Love, we
have nothing but an empty shell.

Time Vs. Love

People will tell you time heals all wounds
Reality is only love does that
Time only fades the pain, never to completely cease
A mother loses her kids, hopping from Doctor to Doctor
In order to obtain more prescription drugs
Her children have no father and now, no mother
Changing schools, changing homes
Growing up to become angry young men.
How does time heal their wounds?
How does time heal their feelings of rejection, suffering, and pain?
Reality is, only love does that

Forgotten

I forgot to pick you up today

Were you scared?

Were you hurt?

Were you lonely?

Standing alone on a busy street

Yet no one casting a second glance

Bills are piling up, business deals gone awry;

no money to keep them at bay.

I can't get the thoughts to stop

I wipe a tear away and pull the trigger

I forgot to pick you up today

Were you scared?

Were you hurt?

Were you lonely?

Love said, "No, not I.

You were the one who was scared

You were the one who was hurt

And you were the one who was lonely.

It was not I."

All Grown Up

She sits on the curb, anxious but patiently waiting
She turns 17; her paycheck feeds all three
She's a mother way too young.
At night, she's restless, waiting for dawn
She wants to see if her mother came home
She goes to school, only to deal with her siblings' problems
Her brother has been expelled; her sister caught smoking in the
Bathroom
She's afraid to tell her mom the news that awaits, angry at the fates
Another night falls, her mother heading again to the bar
Leaving her to be a mother of three, once more.
Her mother has lost her job.
She's scared to tell her step-dad the news
that awaits, angry at the fates.
She's called the police in the midst of the
beatings, hoping they'll come In time
Day in, day out, the cycle continues.
She turns 18 in an empty house, tearfully
wondering what happens next.

Sarah's New Beginning

For six years, Sarah missed her mother
She cried herself to sleep at night, wishing
she could share her life with her.
For six years, Sarah wondered about her brothers and sisters,
What they looked like, how they were.
Sarah had a daughter of her own, and her family was reunited
Two years later, Sarah realizes she never lost anything great.
Her family continues to belittle her and point out her mistakes.
She can't help but wonder, 'Where the hell they were for six years?"
Sarah's sister had a few problems as well
She watched knowingly, as her family washed
their hands of her sister too.
After two years of having her family back, Sarah longs for those
Six years, when she didn't exist.
She smiles as she turns away
Her family once left her alone and scared
Now she walks away, confident and free.

Chapter Two:

Life Is Like A Road

We all take wrong turns and have had to overcome
a few speed bumps. Growing up is no different.
Here are some examples of wrong turns.

Drinking and Driving

The place was eerily quiet considering

that I was going to visit a friend.

No one was around, so I stumbled into the other room.

My eyes were not tired, nor had I been crying.

After all, I was invincible; I was Superman

The place was cold, so dam cold

All of the crew was there, standing around

I craned my neck to see what they were looking at

Melissa, my girlfriend, lay still as can be.

What happened?

How did she get here?

Then I remembered, I had a few too many.

She wanted to drive, but I wouldn't let her

Now here we are, in this place

I'm fine, except my girlfriend's dead

Today is her birthday, sweet 16 she'll be

All I can think is, I wish it were me.

Decisions

Alone, Ashamed, and filled with guilt

Confined by walls that men have built

Fences laced with razors and men with guns

Lying in my cell feeling the wrongs I've done

Wishing I could turn back time

Talk to a younger me and prevent my crime

Days and nights are filled with pain

Hopes of freedom eating at my brain

I'm not a killer, but I made wrong choices

Doing things my way and ignoring the voices

Voices of family and those who cared

Alone and on my own with only the memories we shared

Freedom had now finally come

I'm no longer a number; I am now a name

I look back at all the guilt and pain

To return to that I'd have to be insane

Years have gone by and can never be replaced

Another page in the book I was forced to face

Family and friends happy that I am here

Family and friends who will never know that fear

I sleep at night but still have the dreams

My time is done but never ending it seems

Behind me now is the loneliness and stress

Home from prison and taught a valuable lesson.

Love or Obsession

Why do women love him?

Are they seeking redemption for their souls?

Are they punishing themselves for some unknown cause?

Why do women love him?

Is it excuse's that they love to weave?

Authors of fictional stories they wish to be?

Why do women love him?

He, who is abusive?

He, who is an alcoholic?

He, who is hooked on crack?

Why do women love him?

Are they trying to save a scared little boy?

Are they trying to connect with their past?

Trying to reach their daddy, who is a ghost?

What is it about him that keeps women coming back?

First Time

Do you remember you said

"Baby I love you"

"I promise we'll get married one day"

"You know, you're the only one for me"

"Doing 'it' will only make us closer"

"Jack and Diane are doing it; in fact everyone at school has but us"

"Baby, I'm not gonna wait forever, I

promise you nothing will change"

Why is it on Monday then, you've already forgotten my name?

Fate

In the still of the night, I've made another decision
This decision too, will affect the rest of my life
In the dawn of the morning light, will I
be able to keep my promise?
I love this little baby of mine, my unborn child
I made an unconscious choice nine months ago,
When we failed to use protection
The choice I'm making now, asks so many questions
So many questions unanswered
Why didn't I give more thought to that night,
When we had a few passionate moments.

Pregnancy Tests

I was sixteen when I found out you were coming

Scared was I, yet excited too

Someone to love and hold

Someone who'd give unconditional love to me

I can't believe you're going on eight now

No brothers or sisters do you have though

I've been pregnant five or

Six times

I'm sorry babe; I've lost count

I'm sorry baby; but no brothers or sisters will you have

I'm only twenty-five, yet doctors say no more can I have

My heart is broken

If I got pregnant one more time, I'd definitely keep this baby

You see using protection's not for me.

All of the other times I was pregnant,

The timing was not right for me

I chose abortion as my birth control

It's a woman's right and Medicaid paid for it all

I'm sorry baby, if you don't understand

You'll understand better when you become a woman

Five or six consecutive abortions aren't ridicuous

It's perfectly legal.

Chapter Three:
Here Come The Speed Bumps

Speed bumps are life's little curve balls that we have to overcome.
Leaving us without a say, but helping us
to define that which we will
become.

Never Met Anyone Like You

I've never met anyone like you

You think I'm out of control

You can't force me to do as you say or want.

You call me names; say hurtful things

Frustration, questions, tears; they're all that are left of me

I've never met anyone like you

You should at least care about me,

But you want to claim my blessings instead

You get mad when my misfortunes don't come quickly,

Forgetting about me once they do

I've never met anyone like you

Someone filled with lust, jealousy, and greed

How is it possible I've never met anyone like you?

Woman and Roses

Woman are like roses

On first glance, they are simple beauty

On first glance, they are innocence

Woman are like roses

They have a sweet alluring fragrance

Like roses, they also have thorns

But they go unnoticed, until one stabs you

Sometimes causing you pain, making you bleed

Woman are like roses,

They can captivate you, but also trap you

With the swiftness of how they change from friend to foe

Pastor

Pastor, how sweet thou are
How did you get to be one after all?
Leading hundreds in God's path,
Never showing your flock compassion, mercy, or forgiveness
When I got sick, needing prayers
You and your flock called me, not once
Pastor, how sweet thou are
Your ominent power and wisdom left four without a job
You didn't care
The motives behind this decision clear
Money,Pride and Ignorance
Those are the new commandments
We were all searching for
I guess, instead of loving one another,
We should be judging each other
A house of worship is a safe haven
Where each person can praise God without fear or ridicule
Your house of worship only allows those in that are
deemed worthy by you and your associates
There is constant news coverage about sexual abuse and church
Leaders sexuality
But where is the news coverage about
Pastors stealing believers' faith
Pastor, how sweet thou are.

Worthy News

We all want to protect our children, but
how far are we willing to go?
News stations set up stings in order to capture child predators
Did they give thought to concerned
parents who might try the same?
Or foul play that might ensue to these
parents or their unsuspecting
Families
Once predators found out it was in the name of curiosity
Is the press reporting news or are they just trying to create it
Isn't there enough hatred in this world?
Or has TV, ratings become so much more
important than the lives of
Human beings?

Innocence of Calculating

Rape turns something so beautiful into
something ugly and sinister
The unspoken words and feelings between
two people at their most
Vulnerable becomes a power play
The need to control and dominate versus the will to survive
Now this intimate act is shared with so many
Police,prosecutors,judge and jury
Which of the two is the accused?
Who is the accuser?
More often than it should be, It's too hard to tell
I pray for those who have kept their silence
For the victims who feel that justice is not within reach.

Much Too Soon

Their little voices cry out to me
Causing my soul to hurt
Their little tears are my own
They are children for only so long
This year alone, the number of children gone home;
There aren't enough tears, yet the goodbyes are unyielding
Adults are to teach, guide, and protect
Yet the hands that these children reach for
Are often the same ones that show them heaven
Their final resting place.

Playing House

My niece came to me on her sweet sixteen
She asked, 'Why does my mother hate me?'
With tears in my eyes I replied,
'I'm sorry you don't have the relationship
you desire with your mother
The responsibility and joy of raising a child was more of a burden
That's what happens, when children have children.'

Letter To My Mom

Dear Mom, I don't understand

Why did you abort my brothers and sisters but not me?

Why did you tell me you were having a baby?

I got so excited

Why did you lie and say the baby had died

When all along, you had a doctor do it

I don't understand Mom

If someone gets paid to stop a baby from developing and growing,

Why isn't that murder for hire?

I don't understand Mom

Why them, why not me?

Conversations with My Baby

I saw your picture yesterday

And today you're gone

I saw your heart beating

Today, no more

Eight weeks was the time we've shared

Did you know our time would end?

Until we meet again,

Rest little angel, you're in better hands

Weep no more my baby, sadness is no longer

Laugh my baby, you're in God's hands

Like No Other

When I was young,
Kids my age were dreaming of when
they were finally on their own
Instead I sat and wondered, when my
Mother would walk out on me
When I was young, kids my age thought they were invincible
I had those thoughts, never
Instead I thought that I would die young,
some disease no one knew
I guess in a way, I'm like no other
Now I'm 26, still young, but I thought I'd die younger
I'm a mother now and facing a possible death sentence
Where did my faith go?
I think I could never leave my daughter
How can I leave my husband to raise her all alone?
My body is destroying itself against my will
The name of this disease has been hidden
for some reason or another
My future is put on hold until my body's secret is told
I guess in a way, I really am not like any other

Help

Tears are rolling down my face

I beg you and plead with you to go slower

The steroids are making my legs stronger,

But I still feel vulnerable and weak

I'm supposed to stay here, for as long as it takes

Just do what I know has to be done, without any questions or

Complaints

But my life is not in this hospital

And just because I have M.S., doesn't mean I'm invisible.

Don't Assume

When you see a young woman pull up with handicapped plates

And she jumps out of the car without aid

Don't assume the car's her grandfather's

Don't assume the car's not hers

When you see a young woman trip over her own toes

Don't assume she's clumsy and begin to laugh

When you see a young woman walking with a cane

Don't assume it's part of a fashion decoration

Don't assume she's using it to gain attention

When you meet a young woman living with M.S.

Don't assume she wants your pity

Don't assume she's grateful that you sympathize for her situation

When you meet a young woman living with M.S.

Don't assume she needs your help and rush right in

She may want you to wait until she asks

I'm grateful for my M.S.

It's made me more mentally and emotionally independent

It's made me more mentally and emotionally stronger

It's made my daughter more compassionate and merciful

It's made me learn that when I need help,

people don't mind If I ask

So please don't assume one thing about me

When you see my balance is off

Don't assume I'm drunk

When you see needle marks in my skin

Don't assume I'm an addict

When you see me getting help from the State

Don't assume it's because I don't want to work

Don't assume I have ten children by six

different men sitting at home

When you see me crying

Don't assume I'm feeling sorry for myself

I'm just mourning the life I used to have

When you see a young woman with a disability

Don't assume she has nothing to offer

My life isn't over; It's just changed

I've learned numerous valuable lessons

I know I still have a lot to offer

I consider myself fortunate for this disease

The saying, "Whatever doesn't kill you,

makes you stronger", is true

And If you will just let me, I can prove it to you

Look Around

My hair is a little too long, dirty and unkempt
My clothes are the same ones I've had on since last week
I'm sitting on the corner, needing something hot to eat
People walk past me, even go as far as crossing the street
Just to avoid me, avoid being forced to look at me
But if people took a closer look,
They'd see a son, and architect, even a war veteran
If people took a closer look, they'd see a man
Who If given the chance to work, would have a home

Chapter Four:

Life Goes On

Putting the past behind us is the first step. Move on. You deserve a
second chance. Love can help. All you
have to do is lower your shield.

In Dreams

I never thought my dream would come true,
Until the day I met you.
Something about you came to mind
And stuck in my heart.
Surprised I was, at how I missed you
Met you only once,
And became angry and disappointed
At the thought of not seeing you
It makes no logical sense, I know
But four short weeks later,
The truth in my heart is inescapable.
I'm in love with you

The Path

I was walking down a dirt beaten path one day
It looked as if at least a hundred armies had been here
If there were a way off, the exit was clearly hidden
With no better ideas, I continued on
Out of the corner of my eye.
Something snagged my attention
My heart quickened; my pace picked up in speed
Your love was there for the taking, brighter than a thousand stars
As we walked hand and hand, rocks began to kick up on us
I picked each one up as we continued on.
Through our journeys, well stumble upon a few
We'll just pick them up together and continue through

Beautiful

She is a beautiful woman

The person she is on the inside radiates all the way through

She taught me what it means to love

She taught me that people could change

She taught me that perseverance pays off:

That no one should be left behind

She is a beautiful woman with the ability to forgive

She taught me not to forget but to remember

History has a way of repeating itself

She has touched everyone's life and made me a better person

She gives little of herself to everyone she knows

Some small sliver, to take and carry with us.

Hate to Love You

I don't wanna love you
But it's out of my hands
I don't wanna love you
You've turned my life upside down
I don't wanna love you any longer,
But I can't help myself
We were to be man and wife
But our relationship came to an end
Now here we are, once again
I don't wanna love you
But it's beyond my control
I can't live without you
You're my best friend
My family thinks you're not good for me
And no matter what, I'll keep taking you back
How I wish I could prove them wrong
Cause I don't wanna love you anymore,
But you've stolen my heart
You've made choices, I wish you hadn't
And since then, I've put up a shield
But I wish it could be taken down
I don't wanna love you, but I do
You are my soul mate to the very end.

It's Good with Love

Loving you is wrong,but that's all I want to do

You look into my eyes with a steady gaze

Feelings in secret come tumbling out

Loving you is wrong, but when we touch

Mountains softly quiver

I want to hold you in my arms

Your deepest fears be made known to me

Wake up with me in the morning darling, I'll have coffee on

Let's go to bed in the evening; I want to watch you sleep

Loving you is wrong, but that's all I want to do

If you're sick or hurting, I want to comfort you

Ssshh, don't cry; wipe those tears away.

Im not trying to hurt you; just trying to

prevent more heartache for you.

Loving you is wrong, but that's all I want to do

And in the morning when the sun rises,

we find our love has to end

Know this, no regrets will I have, for I experienced love the way it's

Meant to be

If only for a moment.

If Only

If only I could…

Wipe away just one tear

If only I could…

Make you smile just once today

Then I would know…

I helped ease a little bit of pain that you feel

If only I could…

Take those dark clouds from your eyes

If only I could…

Protect you, just a little

If only I could…

Stand in your dark shadows

If only I could…

Give you back the sun

Then I would know…

I've shown you love

Love like you have always given to me

Chapter Five:
Scars

It all ends with families. Some of us have had it good, while others have been left with scars. Scars are left to remind us not to repeat the lesson twice. With knowledge and understanding, we can move past our trials and tribulations. We can live a life filled with patience and forgiveness for others as well as ourselves.

It's important we don't just dwell on the negative aspects of our lives, but remember that life isn't completely bad.

It holds come comic moments as well. Those lighter moments will help bring us through the tougher time.

Have You Ever Had a Bad Day

I woke up in search of coffee; only to learn none was left

As a new pot is brewing, I go upstairs to get dressed

Only to learn that my favorite jeans are gone.

My wife probably threw them out

Because of the big whole in the knee

On I trudge to Delaware, I must go

An 18-wheeler obscures my view

I can only hope in an easy pass lane, I'm in

No such luck; in the mail, a ticket soon will come

Next stop is the Post Office located next to the police station

As I'm leaving, an officer approaches

"Sir, I have to issue you a ticket; you're parked the wrong way."

That's it, home I'm going; everything there will be in order

In the door I walk and the demands start flying

Fix the sink

Mow the lawn

Take out the trash

Call the electrician

Well at least I'm home, not in the car

Two tickets I've gotten; no chance of getting any more

I greet my son and watch in horror, as he

pukes all over my new Armani

Dinner and bed is now my goal

42

Bless her heart, my wife has made my favorite meal
Just beginning to feel the rest of the evening I'll enjoy
When ding-dongs the door does ring
Dear God you've got to be joking....
It's my mother in law

Ode to the Dirty Diapers

Ode to the dirty diapers,

Whose stench will not clear

Ode to the dirty diapers,

They can transfer a home into an instant open burial ground

Ode to the dirty diapers

For when it's his or her turn, no one seems to be around

Ode to the dirty diapers,

Oops, here comes one now.

Say What

Potty training is so much fun
We sit and sit until we hear a whiz
We sit and sit until we hear a plop
We try to come up with cute little names
for pee and poop and private
Parts
We clap our hands, cheer and shout
We call our families to tell them the news,
who cheer and shout as well
So glad to be done with diapers we are,
That we cannot see what's in store for us next
We take our child to the store and she decides it's time to go
The bathroom is full, but lucky for us, one stall is left
As I wait for my daughter to be done
She hears a noise and loudly asks
"EEEWW Mommy, did you fart?"

Mr. Skunks

I got my cat sometime in September
She was too young to be taken from her mother
I named her Mr. Skunks, cause I was told she was a he
Now I guess, you can call her a she-man
It's no wonder she hates me
Skunks went into heat for the first time last week
And my four-year old wondered what was wrong
I tried telling her Skunks didn't feel well;
she needed to see a doctor
To which my daughter replied,
I'm sick like Skunkies, I need to go to the doctors too'
Time for a different tactic, hopefully one that would work better
Skunks came out of heat after only a week
Thank God, I wasn't ready to get my daughter fixed too.

Family Addition

My mommy's having a baby
Why isn't daddy having one too?
They said the baby's a girl,
But all I can see are cheeks
I think my sister ate something big to make
her cheeks swell up like that
Grandma and Grandpa make a big fuss
They make silly faces and funny noises
I wonder if their faces are gonna stay like that
I guess my sister is okay
She sleeps, eats, and cries
Yeah, I guess my sister's pretty cool
Especially when she laughs at something I do
Still, I think I want a brother

My Daughter

I love the look, texture, and feel of paper
Paper is so clean and begs me to fill it with words
My daughter is a lot like me
Except her words are lines, circles, and shapes
Instead of paper and coloring books,
Walls are her canvases
She appreciates colors, just as I do.
She know the beauty of this world has many colors
She believes in princesses and princes
And happily ever-after, but sometimes, I
know, we must make our own
I hope one day, my words are magical
Changing people's lives in a small degree for the better
My daughter however, does so through her actions
Kids are kids, more playmates to share the fun with
Adults are all nice, no matter what they've done
The concept of strangers hurting her is surreal
When I look at my daughter, I see how truly beautiful she is
She smiles a lot, laughs easily, and gives love freely
I wish we all had the heart of a three-year old.

My Biggest Fan

I held you when you were small,

Your whole hand wrapped around just one of my fingers.

I saw you take your first shaky step,

And I saw you fall.

I picked you up and kissed your boo-boos

I heard your first giggle and your first word

Amazing, how you laughed at the silliest face I make

Or the weirdest sound

You were my biggest fan

I watched you as you left for your first day of school,

With tears in my eyes, I thought, "She's not a baby anymore"

Amazing, how what seems like yesterday,

You were my biggest fan.

Yesterday, you were three; today you're ten.

I watch unbelieving, as you gallantly ride horses,

Gracefully dance, and tend to animals,

With gentle and loving hands

Amazing, how what seems like yesterday

You were my biggest fan

However, that was yesterday

Today, the tides have turned

I see you for the young lady you've become

Look there goes my daughter

And I'm her biggest fan.

Chapter Six:
Phoenix Birds

Through tragedy, we can sometimes see victims that have made
it through. There are still others, who haven't had it good, but
have been able to move on and become something great. This
last chapter is dedicated to all of those who have believed in
something, whether it is themselves or a higher power. This
chapter is dedicated to my belief in God. My life could have
been a tragedy a long time ago, if it weren't for my faith. Let's try
individually and as a whole to make the world a better place.

Jesus Is

I'm working on a replica of your beautiful face

I'm trying so hard; to be perfect, not make a mistake

The colors are so close together,

When it's done, the colors will blend

It will create a picture of love, a picture of peace

I'll send this portrait of you on

Hopefully, it will arrive in time

As I sit here and create,

I think of your wonders

I sit and think, 'what will I learn as I recreate your face'

I've just begun my picture of you

I've just begun to make a few mistakes.

As I continue, my mistakes will go on; the lessons I learn will grow

I'm creating a picture of love, with love in my heart

I know I will see the errors I have and will make

Through your gentle and loving ways;

As I sit and recreate your beautiful face.

Though these mistakes I made are small; others are not

I hope not to mess up so badly that I can't see you.

Although I'm sure, you'll continue to correct and guide me

Through your gentle and loving ways,

As I sit and recreate your beautiful face.

Mom

You carried me and held me for nine
months, even before I was born
You carried me and held me before I could walk
You carried me and held me when I was still a child,
Scraped and battered from falling
You held me and comforted me when I was a young man,
Heartbroken from love gone wrong
For years, you carried me, held me, and comforted
me, through all kinds of storms.
You are more than a mother and a friend,
You are my hero and my inspiration.

A Child's Plea

I'm so mad at you Daddy
I don't want to talk to you
I don't even want to see you again
Why did you leave?
Why did you have to go?
Someone may need your help somewhere, but I need you here
You fought the fire, but it got the best of you
People are calling you a hero who died in the line of duty
But you were a hero already being my daddy

The Soldier

He never saw them, but his sense of honor and faith were great

An army of angels surrounded him as he left home

An army of angels surrounded him as he boarded the plane

An army of angels surrounded him as he

walked the war-torn streets

He never saw them, but his sense of honor and faith were great

An army of angels surrounded him,

Protecting him until it was time to return back home

He never saw their physical embrace

He never knew God's words were left behind

Or that the legion of guardian angels stayed

He never saw them, but his sense of honor and faith were great

He only knew he was blessed and his faith grown stronger

He only knew someone loved him and kept careful watch.

A Letter to You

It's been five years since the Lord took you
away on the day the Towers fell
As I'm raising our family by myself, I
hope your death was not in vein
I thought September 11th was our nation's
wake-up call, yet trouble remains
In public schools, the Pledge of Allegiance can't be said,
Because of one phrase, 'One nation under God'
You and I value beliefs such as freedom, justice, and equality
You and I give no weight to houses, cars, or money
I promise you I won't let your death mean nothing
I promise you our son will know the values we hold dear
Since you died, the world's gone mad
Young men and women are dying daily,
Serving our country; bringing freedom to other countries
The 10 Commandments came under attack
Because it was placed on a courtroom wall
Shouldn't a democracy that believes in
freedom be able to live without fear
Our son really misses you; he needs his dad.
He's getting so big; he just started school.
Spanish is becoming a dominant language in the United States
As a matter of fact, Donovan's class is
teaching them this other language
We are one nation, with only one language, English

Our country is changing, English no longer

being the only dominant language

Yes our country is changing, not necessarily for the better

I miss you so much and I am so scared

As Donovan gets older I wonder if he'll be safe in school

Students are bringing guns to school

And I wonder what type of education will he be getting

Will his intelligence be nurtured or will

he learn that killing solves all

I'll try to write you another letter when I've got time

But know that we really miss you

On your birthday, on our anniversary,

Christmas, and other holidays;

We light a candle

I promise you I won't let your death be in vain

I promise you Donovan will know the values we hold dear

Not the values of God-less terrorists and other people

who feel America is actually getting better this way.

America Dreams

After the September 11th tragedy, I am left without words
My heart lies there without being able to shed a single tear
Fear engulfs me, boundless and without end
I pray for my fellow Americans and the natives of other lands
Will humanity survive?
Will we wither and die?
The terror is man-made, the cause and effect of hatred and rage
Rape, robbery, murder, and despair is all we can see
Children shooting up classmates
The name God being ripped away from societies
Although, it is written on U.S. currency
Hope is dwindling quickly
Will there be another chance?
U.S. lives and breathes terrorism every day
Not just from foreign land, but here on our own soil
We stood together on the 9/11 call
What happened in the time that followed?
United our great U.S. of A. stands, but divided it will fall
We cannot be united against terrorism, if we can't be united here
America dreams of life without wars, yet wishing isn't enough
I dream that one day, the world hears the
bells of freedom ring for all.

www.ingramcontent.com/pod-product-compliance
Lightning Source LLC
Chambersburg PA
CBHW021004150626
46549CB00012BA/1247